HEAR MY CRY

—

WORDS FOR WHEN

THERE ARE NO WORDS

BIBLE
SOCIETY

Bible Society
Trinity Business Centre
Stonehill Green, Westlea
Swindon SN5 7DG
biblesociety.org.uk
bibleresources.org.uk

ISBN: 978-0-564-04923-3

Typesetting and production by Bible Society Resources Ltd,
a wholly-owned subsidiary of The British and Foreign Bible Society
Cover design by Patrick Knowles
Internal design by Colin Hall

Printed in Great Britain
BSRL/2014

Foreword

In this centenary year of the outbreak of the First World War historians will be reviewing once again the causes of the war, debating who was to blame for its outbreak, its bloody protracted course and its effect on the history of the rest of the twentieth century. But these debates mask the real stories of that terrible war – the thoughts, hopes and fears of the ordinary people that fought in the mud and blood of the trenches, or at sea or in the air. War is first and foremost about people, and people are individuals who have to make sense of the circumstances in which they find themselves. In war this can be a huge personal challenge.

Some may choose to argue in the coming months about on whose side was God in the First World War, but that is an arid argument. God does not take sides between countries, however he is passionately concerned for the people who live in those countries and get caught up in war. He made us, He loves us and he wants us to love him in return. In peace or war God is interested in us as individuals.

In this helpful publication are psalms, poems, photos and personal stories that connect those caught up in the turmoil of the Great War with the peace, promise and real purpose in life offered by their loving Heavenly Father. To make sense of war we can do nothing better than place our hope and faith in God and in his Son, Jesus Christ. This publication is a timely guide to help to do just that.

General the Lord Dannatt GCB CBE MC DL
Chief of the General Staff 2006-2009

John 14.27

*Peace is what I leave with you; it is my own peace
that I give you. I do not give it as the world does.
Do not be worried and upset; do not be afraid.*

Contents

Stories

Prayers

Hymns

Paintings

Prayer

Almighty God, our heavenly Father, we remember with thanksgiving
those who made the supreme sacrifice for us in time of war.
We pray that the offering of their lives may not have been in vain.
By your grace enable us this day to dedicate ourselves anew
to the cause of justice, freedom and peace; and give us the
wisdom and strength to build a better world, for the honour and
glory of your name; through Jesus Christ our Lord. Amen.

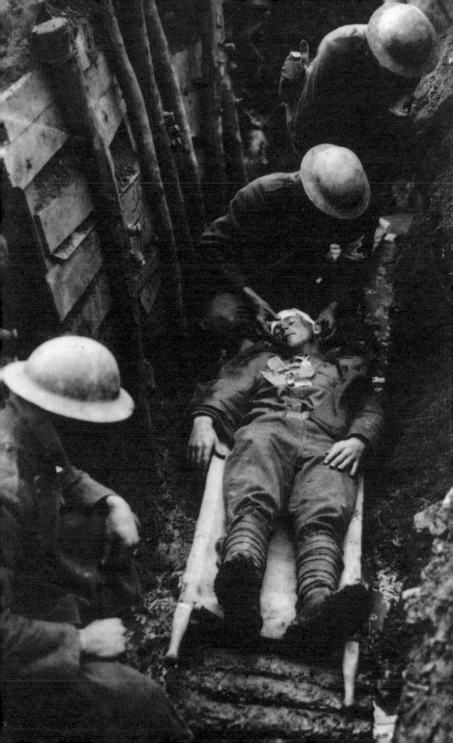

Psalm 3

I HAVE SO MANY ENEMIES, LORD,
    so many who turn against me!
They talk about me and say,
    'God will not help him.'

But you, O Lord, are always my shield from danger;
    you give me victory
and restore my courage.
    I call to the Lord for help,
and from his sacred hill he answers me.

I lie down and sleep,
    and all night long the Lord protects me.
I am not afraid of the thousands of enemies
    who surround me on every side.

Come, Lord! Save me, my God!
    You punish all my enemies
and leave them powerless to harm me.
    Victory comes from the Lord —
may he bless his people.

Psalm 6

LORD, DON'T BE ANGRY AND REBUKE ME!
    Don't punish me in your anger!
I am worn out, O Lord; have pity on me!
    Give me strength; I am completely exhausted
and my whole being is deeply troubled.
    How long, O Lord, will you wait to help me?

Come and save me, Lord;
    in your mercy rescue me from death.
In the world of the dead you are not remembered;
    no one can praise you there.

I am worn out with grief;
    every night my bed is damp from my weeping;
my pillow is soaked with tears.
    I can hardly see;
my eyes are so swollen
    from the weeping caused by my enemies.

Keep away from me, you evil people!
    The Lord hears my weeping;
he listens to my cry for help
    and will answer my prayer.
My enemies will know the bitter shame of defeat;
    in sudden confusion they will be driven away.

Psalm 8

O LORD, OUR LORD,
   your greatness is seen in all the world!
Your praise reaches up to the heavens;
   it is sung by children and babies.
You are safe and secure from all your enemies;
   you stop anyone who opposes you.

When I look at the sky, which you have made,
   at the moon and the stars, which you set in their places —
what are human beings, that you think of them;
   mere mortals, that you care for them?

Yet you made them inferior only to yourself;
   you crowned them with glory and honour.
You appointed them rulers over everything you made;
   you placed them over all creation:
sheep and cattle, and the wild animals too;
   the birds and the fish
and the creatures in the seas.

O Lord, our Lord,
   your greatness is seen in all the world!

A last letter

THEO CHADBURN

13th York and Lancaster Regiment

ON APRIL 9 1918, 29-YEAR-OLD THEO CHADBURN, A MINER FROM
SHEFFIELD, WROTE TO HIS WIFE LILY. HIS LETTERS HOME, ON CREAMY
LINED PAPER, WERE ALL WRITTEN IN PENCIL, AND THEY ENDED WITH A
ROW OF KISSES. THIS WAS TO BE HIS LAST. THREE DAYS LATER HE WAS
KILLED, IT IS THOUGHT WHILE RESCUING COLLEAGUES FROM A BURNING
BUILDING. HIS BODY WAS NEVER FOUND.

Theo was a Sergeant in the 13th Battalion of the York and
Lancaster Regiment, serving in France.

'I am daily thinking of you,' he wrote to Lily and his six-year-old
daughter May, 'and constantly hoping and trusting God for the
reunion, may he grant us that privilege.

'I believe that I have still a work to do for him and my
mind is broader. I believe that every day I learn more of his
goodness and am waiting his pleasure to be able to do a work
for him in conjunction with my dearest wife.'

Heartbreakingly, this letter arrived home after Theo's death. At
first, Lily thought he had been taken prisoner. It was to be a year
later, after the war had ended, in April 1919, that she received a
letter from the War Office. It read,

'It is not thought that any hope can now be entertained that
Sergeant Chadburn has survived and steps will shortly be taken
to consider the question of the presumption of his death.'

Theo, like all his family, was a member of the Salvation Army in Sheffield, and played in the band at weekends. He wrote from the front less than a fortnight before his death of his 'privilege' to be at a Salvation Army meeting.

'The place was packed with soldiers and there were about 150 fellows who made the necessary decision,' he says, of men committing themselves to God.

'I tell you,' he wrote to Lily, 'it was the best Easter Sunday night meeting I have ever spent. I was greatly blessed.'

His tiny black leather-bound diary from 1917 contains a page from Deuteronomy 28, ripped from a larger Bible. It reads,

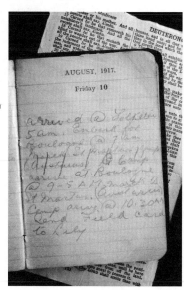

'The Lord shall cause thine enemies that rise up against thee to be smitten before thy face: they shall come out against thee one way and flee before thee seven ways.'

Theo's name is engraved on the Ploegsteert Memorial near Ypres. Lily never remarried.

Psalm 11

I TRUST IN THE LORD FOR SAFETY.

How foolish of you to say to me,
'Fly away like a bird to the mountains,
   because the wicked have drawn their bows and aimed their
           arrows
to shoot from the shadows at good people.
   There is nothing a good person can do
when everything falls apart.'

The Lord is in his holy temple;
   he has his throne in heaven.
He watches people everywhere
   and knows what they are doing.
He examines the good and the wicked alike;
   the lawless he hates with all his heart.

He sends down flaming coals and burning sulphur on the wicked;
   he punishes them with scorching winds.
The Lord is righteous and loves good deeds;
   those who do them will live in his presence.

Psalm 13

HOW MUCH LONGER WILL YOU FORGET ME, LORD?
    FOR EVER?
How much longer will you hide yourself from me?
How long must I endure trouble?
    How long will sorrow fill my heart day and night?
How long will my enemies triumph over me?

Look at me, O Lord my God, and answer me.
    Restore my strength; don't let me die.
Don't let my enemies say, 'We have defeated him.'
    Don't let them gloat over my downfall.

I rely on your constant love;
    I will be glad, because you will rescue me.
I will sing to you, O Lord,
    because you have been good to me.

Psalm 16

PROTECT ME, O GOD; I TRUST IN YOU FOR SAFETY.
 I say to the Lord, 'You are my Lord;
all the good things I have come from you.'

How excellent are the Lord's faithful people!
 My greatest pleasure is to be with them.

Those who rush to other gods
 bring many troubles on themselves.
I will not take part in their sacrifices;
 I will not worship their gods.

You, Lord, are all I have,
 and you give me all I need;
my future is in your hands.
 How wonderful are your gifts to me;
how good they are!

I praise the Lord, because he guides me,
 and in the night my conscience warns me.
I am always aware of the Lord's presence;
 he is near, and nothing can shake me.

And so I am thankful and glad,
 and I feel completely secure,
because you protect me from the power of death.
 I have served you faithfully,
and you will not abandon me to the world of the dead.

You will show me the path that leads to life;
 your presence fills me with joy
and brings me pleasure for ever.

Soldier and poet

CYRIL MEAD

Royal Inniskilling Fusiliers

ALTHOUGH HE GREW UP IN THE VILLAGE OF GOOD EASTER, NEAR CHELMSFORD, CYRIL MEAD WAS CONSCRIPTED INTO AN IRISH REGIMENT, THE ROYAL INNISKILLING FUSILIERS. HE FOUGHT IN FRANCE, MACEDONIA, PALESTINE AND EGYPT.

'His faith was everything to him,' says his son-in-law Anthony Hasler. 'He was active in the village church and was the organist and also the secretary there. His faith sustained him through the war without any doubt at all.'

Cyril wrote poems that he sent to his sister, Sissy. Many express his faith. In one, 'A Trusting Soldier's Prayer', he wrote:

'When death sweeps o'er the battle field
I pray thou wilt thy servant shield'

And in the Bible, written in Satliki, Greece, Cyril claimed the Bible has 'pearls of precious worth':

'Oh may I read with open eyes
And with sincere desire
That God may bless me and bestow on me His Spirit's fire.'

Psalm 19

HOW CLEARLY THE SKY REVEALS GOD'S GLORY!
How plainly it shows what he has done!
Each day announces it to the following day;
each night repeats it to the next.
No speech or words are used,
no sound is heard;
yet their message goes out to all the world
and is heard to the ends of the earth.
God made a home in the sky for the sun;
it comes out in the morning like a happy bridegroom,
like an athlete eager to run a race.
It starts at one end of the sky
and goes across to the other.
Nothing can hide from its heat.

The law of the Lord is perfect;
it gives new strength.
The commands of the Lord are trustworthy,
giving wisdom to those who lack it.
The laws of the Lord are right,
and those who obey them are happy.
The commands of the Lord are just
and give understanding to the mind.
Reverence for the Lord is good;
it will continue for ever.
The judgements of the Lord are just;
they are always fair.
They are more desirable than the finest gold;
they are sweeter than the purest honey.
They give knowledge to me, your servant;
I am rewarded for obeying them.

No one can see his own errors;
    deliver me, Lord, from hidden faults!
Keep me safe, also, from wilful sins;
    don't let them rule over me.
Then I shall be perfect
    and free from the evil of sin.

May my words and my thoughts be acceptable to you,
    O Lord, my refuge and my redeemer!

Psalm 20

    May the God of Jacob protect you!
May he send you help from his Temple
    and give you aid from Mount Zion.
May he accept all your offerings
    and be pleased with all your sacrifices.
May he give you what you desire
    and make all your plans succeed.
Then we will shout for joy over your victory
    and celebrate your triumph by praising our God.
May the Lord answer all your requests.

Now I know that the Lord gives victory to his chosen king;
    he answers him from his holy heaven
and by his power gives him great victories.
    Some trust in their war chariots
and others in their horses,
    but we trust in the power of the Lord our God.
Such people will stumble and fall,
    but we will rise and stand firm.

Give victory to the king, O Lord;
    answer us when we call.

LORD DUNSANY
A dirge of victory

Lift not thy trumpet, Victory, to the sky,
Nor through battalions nor by batteries blow,
But over hollows full of old wire go,
Where among dregs of war the long-dead lie
With wasted iron that the guns passed by.
When they went eastwards like a tide at flow;
There blow thy trumpet that the dead may know,
Who waited for thy coming, Victory.

It is not we that have deserved thy wreath,
They waited there among the towering weeds.
The deep mud burned under the thermite's breath,
And winter cracked the bones that no man heeds:
Hundreds of nights flamed by: the seasons passed.
And thou hast come to them at last, at last!

Psalm 23

THE LORD IS MY SHEPHERD;
I have everything I need.
He lets me rest in fields of green grass
and leads me to quiet pools of fresh water.
He gives me new strength.
He guides me in the right paths,
as he has promised.
Even if I go through the deepest darkness,
I will not be afraid, Lord,
for you are with me.
Your shepherd's rod and staff protect me.

You prepare a banquet for me,
where all my enemies can see me;
you welcome me as an honoured guest
and fill my cup to the brim.
I know that your goodness and love will be with me all my life;
and your house will be my home as long as I live.

HYMN

O God, our help in ages past

O God, our help in ages past,
  our hope for years to come,
    our shelter from the stormy blast,
and our eternal home.

Beneath the shadow of thy throne
  thy saints have dwelt secure;
sufficient is thine arm alone,
    and our defence is sure.

Before the hills in order stood,
  or earth received her frame,
from everlasting thou art God,
    to endless years the same.

A thousand ages in thy sight
  are like an evening gone;
short as the watch that ends the night
    before the rising sun.

Time, like an ever-rolling stream,
  bears all our years away;
they fly forgotten, as a dream
    dies at the opening day.

O God, our help in ages past,
  our hope for years to come,
be thou our guard while troubles last,
    and our eternal home.

Psalm 29

Praise the Lord, you heavenly beings;
  praise his glory and power.
Praise the Lord's glorious name;
  bow down before the Holy One when he appears.

The voice of the Lord is heard on the seas;
  the glorious God thunders,
and his voice echoes over the ocean.
  The voice of the Lord is heard
in all its might and majesty.

The voice of the Lord breaks the cedars,
  even the cedars of Lebanon.
He makes the mountains of Lebanon jump like calves
  and makes Mount Hermon leap like a young bull.

The voice of the Lord makes the lightning flash.
  His voice makes the desert shake;
he shakes the desert of Kadesh.
  The Lord's voice shakes the oaks
and strips the leaves from the trees
  while everyone in his Temple shouts, 'Glory to God!'

The Lord rules over the deep waters;
  he rules as king for ever.
The Lord gives strength to his people
  and blesses them with peace.

Anzac prayer at the Somme

ELVAS JENKINS

Australian Pioneers

UNDER INTENSE BOMBARDMENT AT GALLIPOLI, LANCE CORPORAL ELVAS JENKINS WAS STRUCK DIRECTLY OVER HIS HEART BY A SHRAPNEL BULLET FROM AN EXPLODING SHELL. HE WOULD HAVE DIED INSTANTLY, BUT THE BALL STRUCK HIS BIBLE, THE NEW TESTAMENT HE CARRIED IN HIS SHIRT POCKET.

The Bible saved his life that day, but he did not survive the war. Among the first Anzacs to reach Gallipoli in 1915, he came through the whole of the terrible Gallipoli campaign, only to lay down his life a few months later on the Western Front in France.

Elvas Jenkins was born in Victoria, Australia in 1888. By 1914, he was in love with Jeanie Reid a student of medicine, and had been ordained a Methodist minister. He was 26. Life seemed to be before him.

But, a month later, war broke out and Elvas joined up. On landing at Gallipoli, his 2nd Field Company Australian Engineers quickly set about their assigned tasks: unloading guns and ammunition, constructing a pier, sinking wells to ensure a water supply, constructing trenches and tunnels and dragging artillery up to the battle lines.

Lance Corporal Jenkins was in charge of one of these groups when, on 7 May, a Turkish shell exploded and the pages of his French New Testament (picked up in Alexandria) were pierced.

He was struck directly over his heart. A lead shrapnel bullet hit all the way to Acts. His life spared, Elvas fought on at Gallipoli and was commissioned 2nd Lieutenant.

The Australians then went to the Western Front and took part in the Battle of the Somme. On 19 July 1916, Elvas was in charge of a reconnaissance party determining the precise location of the German trenches, a dangerous assignment.

A deeply committed Christian, Elvas stood and briefly led his men in prayer. He was in the sights of a concealed German sniper. It is said that he stood to deflect gunfire from his men. He was shot and died the next day.

Psalm 30

I PRAISE YOU, LORD, BECAUSE YOU HAVE SAVED ME
  and kept my enemies from gloating over me.
I cried to you for help, O Lord my God,
  and you healed me;
you kept me from the grave.
  I was on my way to the depths below,
but you restored my life.

Sing praise to the Lord,
  all his faithful people!
Remember what the Holy One has done,
  and give him thanks!
His anger lasts only a moment,
  his goodness for a lifetime.
Tears may flow in the night,
  but joy comes in the morning.

I felt secure and said to myself,
  'I will never be defeated.'
You were good to me, Lord;
  you protected me like a mountain fortress.
But then you hid yourself from me,
  and I was afraid.

I called to you, Lord;
  I begged for your help:
'What will you gain from my death?
  What profit from my going to the grave?
Are dead people able to praise you?
  Can they proclaim your unfailing goodness?
Hear me, Lord, and be merciful!
  Help me, Lord!'

You have changed my sadness into a joyful dance;
    you have taken away my sorrow
and surrounded me with joy.
    So I will not be silent;
I will sing praise to you.
    LORD, you are my God,
I will give you thanks for ever.

C H SORLEY

When you see millions of the mouthless dead

When you see millions of the mouthless dead
Across your dreams in pale battalions go,
Say not soft things as other men have said,
That you'll remember. For you need not so.
Give them not praise. For, deaf, how should they know
It is not curses heaped on each gashed head?
Nor tears. Their blind eyes see not your tears flow.
Nor honour. It is easy to be dead.
Say only this, 'They are dead.' Then add thereto,
'Yet many a better one has died before.'
Then, scanning all the overcrowded mass, should you
Perceive one face that you loved heretofore,
It is a spook. None wears the face you knew.
Great death has made all this for evermore.

EDWARD DE STEIN
Envoi

How shall I say goodbye to you, wonderful, terrible days,
If I should live to live and leave 'neath an alien soil
You, my men, who taught me to walk with a smile in the ways
Of the valley of shadows, taught me to know you and love you,
    and toil
Glad in the glory of fellowship, happy in misery, strong
In the strength that laughs at its weakness, laughs at its sorrows
    and fears,
Facing thee world that was not too kind with a jest and a song?
What can the world hold afterwards worthy of laughter or tears?

Psalm 32

HAPPY ARE THOSE WHOSE SINS ARE FORGIVEN,
   whose wrongs are pardoned.
Happy is the one whom the Lord does not accuse of doing wrong
   and who is free from all deceit.

When I did not confess my sins,
   I was worn out from crying all day long.
Day and night you punished me, Lord;
   my strength was completely drained,
as moisture is dried up by the summer heat.

Then I confessed my sins to you;
   I did not conceal my wrongdoings.
I decided to confess them to you,
   and you forgave all my sins.

So all your loyal people should pray to you in times of need;
   when a great flood of trouble comes rushing in,
it will not reach them.
   You are my hiding place;
you will save me from trouble.
   I sing aloud of your salvation,
because you protect me.

The Lord says, 'I will teach you the way you should go;
   I will instruct you and advise you.
Don't be stupid like a horse or a mule,
   which must be controlled with a bit and bridle
to make it submit.'

The wicked will have to suffer,
but those who trust in the Lord
are protected by his constant love.
You that are righteous, be glad and rejoice
because of what the Lord has done.
You that obey him, shout for joy!

Prayer

Heavenly Father, whose heart is selfless love,
take pity on our divided world;
and grant that we may follow in the steps of your Son
in giving ourselves to the service of others
and reaching out to the marginalized and the despised,
that peace and justice may triumph
and your kingdom come on earth.
In Christ's name we pray.
Amen.

Psalm 34

I WILL ALWAYS THANK THE LORD;
    I will never stop praising him.
I will praise him for what he has done;
    may all who are oppressed listen and be glad!
Proclaim with me the Lord's greatness;
    let us praise his name together!

I prayed to the Lord, and he answered me;
    he freed me from all my fears.
The oppressed look to him and are glad;
    they will never be disappointed.
The helpless call to him, and he answers;
    he saves them from all their troubles.
His angel guards those who honour the Lord
    and rescues them from danger.

Find out for yourself how good the Lord is.
    Happy are those who find safety with him.
Honour the Lord, all his people;
    those who obey him have all they need.
Even lions go hungry for lack of food,
    but those who obey the Lord lack nothing good.

Come, my young friends, and listen to me,
    and I will teach you to honour the Lord.
Would you like to enjoy life?
    Do you want long life and happiness?
Then hold back from speaking evil
    and from telling lies.
Turn away from evil and do good;
    strive for peace with all your heart.

The Lord watches over the righteous
and listens to their cries;
but he opposes those who do evil,
so that when they die, they are soon forgotten.
The righteous call to the Lord, and he listens;
he rescues them from all their troubles.
The Lord is near to those who are discouraged;
he saves those who have lost all hope.

Good people suffer many troubles,
but the Lord saves them from them all;
the Lord preserves them completely;
not one of their bones is broken.
Evil will kill the wicked;
those who hate the righteous will be punished.

The Lord will save his people;
those who go to him for protection will be spared.

Psalm 46

GOD IS OUR SHELTER AND STRENGTH,
always ready to help in times of trouble.
So we will not be afraid, even if the earth is shaken
and mountains fall into the ocean depths;
even if the seas roar and rage,
and the hills are shaken by the violence.

There is a river that brings joy to the city of God,
to the sacred house of the Most High.
God is in that city, and it will never be destroyed;
at early dawn he will come to its aid.
Nations are terrified, kingdoms are shaken;
God thunders, and the earth dissolves.

The Lord Almighty is with us;
the God of Jacob is our refuge.

Come and see what the Lord has done.
See what amazing things he has done on earth.
He stops wars all over the world;
he breaks bows, destroys spears,
and sets shields on fire.
'Stop fighting,' he says, 'and know that I am God,
supreme among the nations,
supreme over the world.'

The Lord Almighty is with us;
the God of Jacob is our refuge.

ALAN SEEGER
Rendezvous

I have a rendezvous with Death
At some disputed barricade,
When Spring comes back with rustling shade
And apple-blossoms fill the air —
I have a rendezvous with Death
When Spring brings back blue days and fair.

It may be he shall take my hand
And lead me into his dark land
And close my eyes and quench my breath —
It may be I shall pass him still.
I have a rendezvous with Death
On some scarred slope of battered hill,
When Spring comes round again this year
And the first meadow-flowers appear.

God knows 'twere better to be deep
Pillowed in silk and scented down,
Where love throbs out in blissful sleep,
Pulse nigh to pulse, and breath to breath,
Where hushed awakenings are dear...
But I've a rendezvous with Death
At midnight in some flaming town,
When Spring trips north again this year,
And I to my pledged word am true,
I shall not fail that rendezvous.

Psalm 54

SAVE ME BY YOUR POWER, O GOD;
    set me free by your might!
Hear my prayer, O God;
    listen to my words!
Proud men are coming to attack me;
    cruel men are trying to kill me —
men who do not care about God.

But God is my helper.
    The Lord is my defender.
May God use their own evil to punish my enemies.
    He will destroy them because he is faithful.

I will gladly offer you a sacrifice, O Lord;
    I will give you thanks
because you are good.
    You have rescued me from all my troubles,
and I have seen my enemies defeated.

Psalm 57

BE MERCIFUL TO ME, O GOD, BE MERCIFUL,
  because I come to you for safety.
In the shadow of your wings I find protection
  until the raging storms are over.

I call to God, the Most High,
  to God, who supplies my every need.
He will answer from heaven and save me;
  he will defeat my oppressors.
God will show me his constant love and faithfulness.

  I am surrounded by enemies,
who are like lions hungry for human flesh.
  Their teeth are like spears and arrows;
their tongues are like sharp swords.

  Show your greatness in the sky, O God,
and your glory over all the earth.

  My enemies have spread a net to catch me;
I am overcome with distress.
  They dug a pit in my path,
but fell into it themselves.

  I have complete confidence, O God;
I will sing and praise you!
  Wake up, my soul!
Wake up, my harp and lyre!
  I will wake up the sun.
I will thank you, O Lord, among the nations.
  I will praise you among the peoples.
Your constant love reaches the heavens;
  your faithfulness touches the skies.
Show your greatness in the sky, O God,
  and your glory over all the earth.

Psalm 63

O GOD, YOU ARE MY GOD,
    and I long for you.
My whole being desires you;
    like a dry, worn-out, and waterless land,
my soul is thirsty for you.
    Let me see you in the sanctuary;
let me see how mighty and glorious you are.
    Your constant love is better than life itself,
and so I will praise you.
    I will give you thanks as long as I live;
I will raise my hands to you in prayer.
    My soul will feast and be satisfied,
and I will sing glad songs of praise to you.

As I lie in bed, I remember you;
    all night long I think of you,
because you have always been my help.
    In the shadow of your wings I sing for joy.
I cling to you,
    and your hand keeps me safe.

Those who are trying to kill me
    will go down into the world of the dead.
They will be killed in battle,
    and their bodies eaten by wolves.
Because God gives him victory,
    the king will rejoice.
Those who make promises in God's name will praise him,
    but the mouths of liars will be shut.

W N HODGSON

Before action

By all the glories of the day
And the cool evening's benison
By that last sunset touch that lay
Upon the hills when day was done,
By beauty lavishly outpoured
And blessings carelessly received,
By all the days that I have lived
Make me a soldier, Lord.

By all of all man's hopes and fears
And all the wonders poets sing,
The laughter of unclouded years,
And every sad and lovely thing;
By the romantic ages stored
With high endeavour that was his,
By all his mad catastrophes
Make me a man, O Lord.

I, that on my familiar hill
Saw with uncomprehending eyes
A hundred of thy sunsets spill
Their fresh and sanguine sacrifice,
Ere the sun swings his noonday sword
Must say good-bye to all of this; —
By all delights that I shall miss,
Help me to die, O Lord.

Psalm 67

GOD, BE MERCIFUL TO US AND BLESS US;
    look on us with kindness,
so that the whole world may know your will;
    so that all nations may know your salvation.

May the peoples praise you, O God;
    may all the peoples praise you!

May the nations be glad and sing for joy,
    because you judge the peoples with justice
and guide every nation on earth.

May the peoples praise you, O God;
    may all the peoples praise you!

The land has produced its harvest;
    God, our God, has blessed us.
God has blessed us;
    may all people everywhere honour him.

Prayer

Gracious Father,
we pray for peace in our world:
for all national leaders
that they may have wisdom to know and courage to do
what is right;
for all men and women
that their hearts may be turned to yourself
in the search for righteousness and truth;
for those who are working to improve international
relationships,
that they may find the true way of reconciliation;
for those who suffer as a result of war:
the injured and disabled,
the mentally distressed,
the homeless and hungry,
those who mourn for their dead,
and especially for those who are without hope or friend
to sustain them in their grief.
Amen.

Through the wire

HARRY FOSTER

York and Lancaster Regiment

LETTER FROM THE SOMME, AUGUST 1916 FROM 20-YEAR-OLD HARRY FOSTER TO HIS MOTHER:

'The Germans sent out bombing parties…and tried to bomb us out of their front line. For five hours we kept them at bay, having only those bombs which were carried by each man (two apiece).

'When these had all been collected and exhausted, we managed to find a German bomb-store, and used their own bombs against them.

'These lasted another hour or so, but we had to eventually give ground and retire along the trench.

'Things began to look serious, as we had no bombs left and we were receiving showers of them from the Germans. It was pretty evident that nothing could be done and it was a case of every man for himself, or surrender and be captured. Of course, there was not the slightest doubt as to which course we should take, so we all commenced to run the gauntlet across No Man's Land back to our trenches.

'We had 400 yards to go and immediately a terrific machine gun fire was opened on us. I cannot write about the scene that followed. It was simply awful.

'I could see it was absolutely useless in going on and I immediately threw myself into a shell hole a few yards from the German trench, amongst the remains of their wire entanglements.

'One or two others followed my example and immediately dropped in, but the Germans had seen them and they commenced throwing bombs at us from their trench.

'There was nothing for it but to shift and most of us made another dash. I looked ahead and saw another shell hole about 10 yards away and stopping low, I dashed for it.

'I was in a terrible plight, as weak as a rat and not knowing what to do. I decided to wait until it was dark, when I should have a better chance of crawling back to our trenches.

'At last I knew it was getting dark as the rays of a star shell managed to penetrate the dark corner where I was. Making as little movement as possible, I slipped off my equipment and everything else I was carrying and commenced to crawl through the shattered wire. Several times I got hung up on it and it seemed ages before I could free myself.

'At last I got clear of the wire which stretched about 30 yards or more and began to breathe freely. I got back to our lines and at once went to the dressing station and had my arms, wrists, hands and knees painted with iodine to prevent any poisoning from the many barbed wire scratches I had.

'Through God's help alone I survived that day. All through, you can see how wonderfully our prayers were answered and I am, as I know you are, full of gratitude to Him.'

Harry was one of two men left alive and without serious wounds from his platoon of 36 men.

Psalm 70

SAVE ME, O GOD!
    Lord, help me now!
May those who try to kill me
    be defeated and confused.
May those who are happy because of my troubles
    be turned back and disgraced.
May those who jeer at me
    be dismayed by their defeat.

May all who come to you
    be glad and joyful.
May all who are thankful for your salvation
    always say, 'How great is God!'

I am weak and poor;
    come to me quickly, O God.
You are my saviour, O Lord —
    hurry to my aid!

VERA BRITTAIN
Perhaps

Perhaps some day the sun will shine again,
And I shall see that still the skies are blue,
And feel once more I do not live in vain,
Although bereft of You.

Perhaps the golden meadows at my feet
Will make the sunny hours of spring seem gay,
And I shall find the white May-blossoms sweet,
Though You have passed away.

Perhaps the summer woods will shimmer bright,
And crimson roses once again be fair,
And autumn harvest fields a rich delight,
Although You are not there.

Perhaps some day I shall not shrink in pain
To see the passing of the dying year,
And listen to the Christmas songs again,
Although You cannot hear.

But though kind Time may many joys renew,
There is one greatest joy I shall not know
Again, because my heart for loss of You
Was broken, long ago.

RUDYARD KIPLING

The verdicts

Not in the thick of the fight,
Not in the press of the odds,
Do the heroes come to their height,
Or we know the demi-gods.

That stands over till peace.
We can only perceive
Men returned from the seas,
Very grateful for leave.

They grant us sudden days
Snatched from their business of war;
But we are too close to appraise
What manner of men they are.

And, whether their names go down
With age-kept victories,
Or whether they battle and drown
Unreckoned, is hid from our eyes.

They are too near to be great,
But our children shall understand
When and how our fate
Was changed, and by whose hand.

Our children shall measure their worth.
We are content to be blind …
But we know that we walk on a new-born earth
With the saviours of mankind.

Psalm 88

LORD GOD, MY SAVIOUR, I CRY OUT ALL DAY,
    and at night I come before you.
Hear my prayer;
    listen to my cry for help!

So many troubles have fallen on me
    that I am close to death.
I am like all others who are about to die;
    all my strength is gone.
I am abandoned among the dead;
    I am like the slain lying in their graves,
those you have forgotten completely,
    who are beyond your help.
You have thrown me into the depths of the tomb,
    into the darkest and deepest pit.
Your anger lies heavy on me,
    and I am crushed beneath its waves.

You have caused my friends to abandon me;
    you have made me repulsive to them.
I am closed in and cannot escape;
    my eyes are weak from suffering.
Lord, every day I call to you
    and lift my hands to you in prayer.

Do you perform miracles for the dead?
    Do they rise up and praise you?
Is your constant love spoken of in the grave
    or your faithfulness in the place of destruction?
Are your miracles seen in that place of darkness
    or your goodness in the land of the forgotten?

Lord, I call to you for help;
    every morning I pray to you.
Why do you reject me, Lord?
    Why do you turn away from me?
Ever since I was young, I have suffered and been near death;
    I am worn out from the burden of your punishments.
Your furious anger crushes me;
    your terrible attacks destroy me.
All day long they surround me like a flood;
    they close in on me from every side.
You have made even my closest friends abandon me,
    and darkness is my only companion.

Psalm 90

O LORD, YOU HAVE ALWAYS BEEN OUR HOME.
　Before you created the hills
or brought the world into being,
　you were eternally God,
and will be God for ever.

You tell us to return to what we were;
　you change us back to dust.
A thousand years to you are like one day;
　they are like yesterday, already gone,
like a short hour in the night.
　You carry us away like a flood;
we last no longer than a dream.
　We are like weeds that sprout in the morning,
that grow and burst into bloom,
　then dry up and die in the evening.

We are destroyed by your anger;
    we are terrified by your fury.
You place our sins before you,
    our secret sins where you can see them.

Our life is cut short by your anger;
    it fades away like a whisper.
Seventy years is all we have —
    eighty years, if we are strong;
yet all they bring us is trouble and sorrow;
    life is soon over, and we are gone.

Who has felt the full power of your anger?
    Who knows what fear your fury can bring?
Teach us how short our life is,
    so that we may become wise.

How much longer will your anger last?
    Have pity, O Lord, on your servants!
Fill us each morning with your constant love,
    so that we may sing and be glad all our life.
Give us now as much happiness as the sadness you gave us
    during all our years of misery.
Let us, your servants, see your mighty deeds;
    let our descendants see your glorious might.
Lord our God, may your blessings be with us.
    Give us success in all we do!

In the presence of God

WALTER CULLIFORD

London Regiment (Queen Victoria's Rifles)

TWENTY-TWO YEAR-OLD WALTER CULLIFORD JOINED THE 9TH LONDON REGIMENT (QUEEN VICTORIA'S RIFLES) IN 1915. AS WELL AS FIGHTING IN FRANCE, HE SPENT TIME IN SALONICA, EGYPT AND ISRAEL. WHEN IN TRAINING IN FOVANT, HE LEARNED MORE ABOUT THE CHRISTIAN FAITH INTO WHICH HE HAD BEEN BORN. IT WAS THIS, HE SAID, THAT SUSTAINED HIM DURING THE NEXT THREE YEARS. 'IT WAS A TIME OF QUIET, HAPPY GROWTH IN SPIRITUAL MATTERS, A PREPARATION FOR THE DAYS WHICH WERE TO COME.'

In his diaries he described his experiences in France as being 'far from pleasant', going 'over the top' 13 times. In Egypt, he acted as escort to a ration caravan of 600 camels and covered 120 miles a week delivering food to the troops. In Salonica he said, 'Marching was hard. Most of the time there was no road'. He covered 1,300 miles during the war.

His daughter Violet says, 'He saw real horrors: men falling dead on either side of him and trampling over their bodies. He recalls several near misses when he should have died.'

And in his diary, Walter wrote that he had 'always had a great horror of warfare' and so 'was not one of the first to rush to the colours'.

Walter's memoirs show that he felt close to God during the war. In Egypt he joined small groups of men holding services in the dark, gathering under the stars to pray and to read the Bible.

'In the quiet of a desert evening by starlight we felt verily in the presence of God and were loath to return to the medlay [sic] of the camp.'

He adds,

'I was never wounded throughout the whole of my service and I did not spend a single day in hospital and I rarely needed any medical attention at all. Truly "the everlasting arms of God were my refuge, my home and underneath were the everlasting arms".'

Violet remembers a particular sadness. 'There was a long period of time when he didn't have any fellowship at all. He had one friend who prayed with him. One night this man committed his life to God and was killed the next day. I think that was a very deep blow to my father who didn't make friends easily.'

56 *Hear my cry*

W B YEATS

An Irish airman foresees his death

I know that I shall meet my fate
Somewhere among the clouds above;
Those that I fight I do not hate
Those that I guard I do not love;
My country is Kiltartan Cross,
My countrymen Kiltartan's poor,
No likely end could bring them loss
Or leave them happier than before.
Nor law, nor duty bade me fight,
Nor public man, nor cheering crowds,
A lonely impulse of delight
Drove to this tumult in the clouds;
I balanced all, brought all to mind,
The years to come seemed waste of breath,
A waste of breath the years behind
In balance with this life, this death.

Psalm 91

WHOEVER GOES TO THE LORD FOR SAFETY,
    whoever remains under the protection of the Almighty,
can say to him,
    'You are my defender and protector.
You are my God; in you I trust.'
    He will keep you safe from all hidden dangers
and from all deadly diseases.
    He will cover you with his wings;
you will be safe in his care;
    his faithfulness will protect and defend you.
You need not fear any dangers at night
    or sudden attacks during the day
or the plagues that strike in the dark
    or the evils that kill in daylight.

A thousand may fall dead beside you,
    10,000 all round you,
but you will not be harmed.
    You will look and see
how the wicked are punished.

You have made the Lord your defender,
    the Most High your protector,
and so no disaster will strike you,
    no violence will come near your home.
God will put his angels in charge of you
    to protect you wherever you go.
They will hold you up with their hands
    to keep you from hurting your feet on the stones.
You will trample down lions and snakes,
    fierce lions and poisonous snakes.

God says, 'I will save those who love me
    and will protect those who acknowledge me as Lord.
When they call to me, I will answer them;
    when they are in trouble, I will be with them.
I will rescue them and honour them.
    I will reward them with long life;
I will save them.'

Hymn

Lead us, heavenly Father, lead us
O'er the world's tempestuous sea;
Guard us, guide us, keep us, feed us,
For we have no help but thee;
Yet possessing every blessing
If our God our Father be.

Saviour, breathe forgiveness o'er us,
All our weakness thou dost know;
Thou didst tread this earth before us,
Thou didst feel its keenest woe;
Self denying, death defying,
Thou to Calvary didst go.

Spirit of our God, descending,
Fill our hearts with heavenly joy;
Love with every passion blending,
Pleasure that can never cloy;
Thus provided, pardoned, guided,
Nothing can our peace destroy.

ROBERT PALMER

How long, O Lord

How long, O Lord, how long, before the flood
Of crimson-welling carnage shall abate?
From sodden plains in West and East, the blood
Of kindly men steams up in mists of hate,
Polluting Thy clean air; and nations great
In reputation of the arts that bind
The world with hopes of heaven, sink to the state
Of brute barbarians, whose ferocious mind
Gloats o'er the bloody havoc of their kind,
Not knowing love or mercy. Lord, how long
Shall Satan in high places lead the blind
To battle for the passions of the strong?
Oh, touch Thy children's hearts, that they may know
Hate their most hateful, pride their deadliest foe.

Psalm 98

SING A NEW SONG TO THE LORD;
 he has done wonderful things!
By his own power and holy strength
 he has won the victory.
The Lord announced his victory;
 he made his saving power known to the nations.
He kept his promise to the people of Israel
 with loyalty and constant love for them.
All people everywhere have seen the victory of our God.

Sing for joy to the Lord, all the earth;
 praise him with songs and shouts of joy!
Sing praises to the Lord!
 Play music on the harps!
Blow trumpets and horns,
 and shout for joy to the Lord, our king.

Roar, sea, and every creature in you;
 sing, earth, and all who live on you!
Clap your hands, you rivers;
 you hills, sing together with joy before the Lord,
because he comes to rule the earth.
 He will rule the peoples of the world
with justice and fairness.

Full marks to the Salvation Army

TROOPER GEORGE JAMESON

1st Battalion, Northumberland Hussars

I'd give full marks to the Salvation Army. They had one place I used to drop into often. And it was a most uncomfortable spot to be in. It was at Vimy. The main road came through Vimy and down on to the plain that way. Well, you didn't take that main road if you could avoid it, it was under constant shellfire. At night it got even worse, as the Germans reckoned that transport used it at night, so they would keep strafing it the whole time. But tucked into the side of the hill was the Salvation Army. And they used to have tea and whatever going all hours of the day. How they survived there I don't know. Wonderful people. In the middle of nowhere to suddenly walk into a place and get a piping hot pot of tea, it was a great reviver.

Parable of the Blind, 1568

PIETER BRUEGEL

Bruegel's terrifying image was painted nearly four centuries before World War One broke out but it has much to say about that war. In the Second World War, leaders and people knew what they were doing: we had a moral duty to defeat Hitler. But the First World War? Why did it begin? Every leader seemed to feel that his country was being attacked and so led his people into aggressive 'defence'. The glory of battle was blinding.

'If the blind lead the blind, both fall into the ditch.' Or the trench. The horrors of trench warfare and its effects upon the human spirit are shown here in the plight of these wretched beggars. They have left behind the security of the village. They cannot see the church, close to them as it is, reaching up to heaven, offering the welcome of many windows and doors. This state of human degradation is the effect of the blindness of war.

Ironically, there is a photograph from the First World War showing a line of men blinded by poison gas (see page 115). It reminds me of this painting, yet those heroic wounded walk straight. They have a leader who sees and who is leading them to healing.

Sister Wendy Beckett

Kit Inspection, 1923–32

SIR STANLEY SPENCER

The artist Sir Stanley Spencer recalled his wartime experiences as a volunteer with the Royal Army Medical Corps in a poignant series of canvases, which depict scenes from daily life and honour the 'forgotten dead' of the First World War. Commissioned for Sandham Memorial Chapel, Hampshire, *Kit Inspection* (a detail from the North Wall) is set at the camp near Farnham where Spencer trained before leaving for the Macedonian Front.

With the Rainbow, 1917

PAUL KLEE

There were two significant effects of the war on the German artist Paul Klee. First was a greater propulsion towards abstraction: 'One deserts the realm of the here and now to transfer one's activity into a realm of the yonder… The more horrible this world, the more abstract our art.' The second was the eventual protection from the front, as too many artists were being killed. *With the Rainbow* was painted in 1917 when Klee was a clerk at a flying school and given a small room in which to continue his painting.

68 *Hear my cry*

The Corn Field, 1918

BY JOHN NASH

John Nash was one of the many young artists throughout Europe who were caught up in the First World War. He experienced the trenches as a soldier until late 1917 when his elder brother Paul Nash, who was a war artist, arranged for John also to become a war artist. They were still in the trenches, not to fight but to make sketches of what they saw.

A few months before the war ended in 1918 the brothers went home to turn these sketches into complete works of art. Both painted terrible depictions of warfare. But when a war ends, if there is still bitterness and anguish, it has not ended. In that same year John Nash drew a great line under 'the pure murder' of the last four years. He drew that line by painting *The Corn Field*.

It is not a nostalgic picture looking back to the world before the war. Rather, I think, it expresses what Nash felt should succeed the war. It is an image of absolute peace. Where war is chaotic and noisy, here all is ordered and silent. There are fruitful harvests. Everywhere there is space and sunlight. There is no fear, only hope and tranquility.

We know, very sadly, that this spiritual state was not, in fact, the result of the war. Perhaps John Nash knew it too because harmony, confidence and freedom come from a change of heart, and the human heart is slow to change. But he hoped.

Sister Wendy Beckett

If wrong was to be resisted

PRIVATE GODFREY BUXTON

Royal Army Medical Corps

During that time one was naturally trying to find out what the Bible said, and it was interesting to find out how many battles in the Old Testament were 'by the word of the Lord'. And in the New Testament neither John the Baptist nor Our Lord ever said anything against a soldier – only told them to do their job within the limits of war. These things in my young mind built up to a confidence that if death was abroad, if wrong was to be resisted, a Christian should be right in amongst it.

Psalm 100

SING TO THE LORD, ALL THE WORLD!
  Worship the Lord with joy;
come before him with happy songs!

Acknowledge that the Lord is God.
  He made us, and we belong to him;
we are his people, we are his flock.

Enter the temple gates with thanksgiving,
  go into its courts with praise.
Give thanks to him and praise him.

The Lord is good;
  his love is eternal
and his faithfulness lasts for ever.

In Flanders fields

JOHN MCCRAE

In Flanders fields the poppies blow
Between the crosses, row on row,
That mark our place; and in the sky
The larks, still bravely singing, fly
Scarce heard amid the guns below.

We are the Dead. Short days ago
We lived, felt dawn, saw sunset glow,
Loved and were loved, and now we lie
In Flanders fields.

Take up our quarrel with the foe:
To you from failing hands we throw
The torch; be yours to hold it high.
If ye break faith with us who die
We shall not sleep, though poppies grow
In Flanders fields.

Words for when there are no words

Psalm 103

PRAISE THE LORD, MY SOUL!
  All my being, praise his holy name!
Praise the Lord, my soul,
  and do not forget how kind he is.
He forgives all my sins
  and heals all my diseases.
He keeps me from the grave
  and blesses me with love and mercy.
He fills my life with good things,
  so that I stay young and strong like an eagle.

The Lord judges in favour of the oppressed
  and gives them their rights.
He revealed his plans to Moses
  and let the people of Israel see his mighty deeds.
The Lord is merciful and loving,
  slow to become angry and full of constant love.
He does not keep on rebuking;
  he is not angry for ever.
He does not punish us as we deserve
  or repay us according to our sins and wrongs.
As high as the sky is above the earth,
  so great is his love for those who honour him.
As far as the east is from the west,
  so far does he remove our sins from us.
As a father is kind to his children,
  so the Lord is kind to those who honour him.
He knows what we are made of;
  he remembers that we are dust.

As for us, our life is like grass.
We grow and flourish like a wild flower;
then the wind blows on it, and it is gone —
no one sees it again.
But for those who honour the Lord, his love lasts for ever,
and his goodness endures for all generations
of those who are true to his covenant
and who faithfully obey his commands.

The Lord placed his throne in heaven;
he is king over all.
Praise the Lord, you strong and mighty angels,
who obey his commands,
who listen to what he says.
Praise the Lord, all you heavenly powers,
you servants of his, who do his will!
Praise the Lord, all his creatures
in all the places he rules.
Praise the Lord, my soul!

A Christian service for prisoners of war

WALTER YOUNG

London Regiment (Post Office Rifles)

WALTER YOUNG'S NEW TESTAMENT FALLS OPEN AT ROMANS 12 TO
VERSES HE READ REGULARLY TO HIS FAMILY AFTER THE WAR, VERSES
WHICH ALSO SUSTAINED HIM DURING THE WAR.

'Hate what is evil, hold onto what is good. Love one another
warmly as Christian brothers and be eager to show respect
for one another. Work hard and do not be lazy. Let your
hope keep you joyful, be patient in your troubles and pray at
all times … Ask God to bless those who persecute you – yes,
ask him to bless, not to curse.'

The New Testament had been given to him by his church,
Woodbridge Chapel in Clerkenwell, and is inscribed with the
message: 'Heaven and earth shall pass away. My word shall not
pass away' (Matthew 24.35). It is still in his family today.

Twenty-five-year-old Walter, a post-office sorter, was against
violence but eventually enlisted in 1915 and fought at the Somme,
Ypres and Passchendaele. He wrote a memoir about his capture
by the Germans and the terrible conditions he endured when he
was put to work as a prisoner of war in a Prussian coal mine.

'This was about the most miserable period of my life,' he
wrote of his time in the mines. 'True, life in the dirtiest and
most dangerous trenches was worse while it lasted, but there
was always the relief to look forward to if one survived. But
life for me at this mine seemed one long round of almost

unbroken misery with hardly anything to relieve it.'

Yet it was here that Walter felt God was saying to him that his fellow PoWs were 'sheep without a shepherd'. So he asked a German officer for permission to hold a

service. It was granted. A series of services, using Walter's little New Testament, were held in the ablutions room where the men washed on leaving the mine. Walter later recalled the first service.

'All the accommodation was occupied and some were standing and the congregation included not only British but Frenchmen and Russians as well. I suppose we numbered about 40 in all. It was a strange scene for a service. There was only one light and that was partially obscured by the steam from some boiler, which made a fairly loud hissing noise all the time. Nobody had a hymn book and it was obvious that only a very few well-known hymns could be chosen. So from my prayer book hymnary I read out the words, verse by verse and most of them joined in the singing which was led by a violin player. It was a very simple Gospel service. I spoke a few words.

'If anything was attempted with a feeling of unfitness and inadequacy surely it was these few services. But possibly that very feeling of weakness was my greatest strength, for I could place no dependence on myself or on others.'

Walter was released at the end of the war.

Words for when there are no words 77

Psalm 113

PRAISE THE LORD!

You servants of the Lord,
    praise his name!
May his name be praised,
    now and for ever.
From the east to the west
    praise the name of the Lord!
The Lord rules over all nations;
    his glory is above the heavens.

There is no one like the Lord our God.
    He lives in the heights above,
but he bends down
    to see the heavens and the earth.
He raises the poor from the dust;
    he lifts the needy from their misery
and makes them companions of princes,
    the princes of his people.
He honours the childless wife in her home;
    he makes her happy by giving her children.

Praise the Lord!

Prayer

Give us courage, O Lord, to stand up and be counted,
to stand up for those who cannot stand up for themselves,
to stand up for ourselves when it is needful for us to do so.
Let us fear nothing more than we fear Thee.
Let us love nothing more than we love Thee,
for thus we shall fear nothing also.
Let us have no other God before Thee,
whether nation or party or state or church.
Let us seek no other peace but the peace which is Thine,
and make us its instruments,
opening our eyes and our ears and our hearts,
so that we should know always what work of peace
we may do for Thee.
Amen.

Psalm 116

I LOVE THE LORD, BECAUSE HE HEARS ME;
    he listens to my prayers.
He listens to me
    every time I call to him.
The danger of death was all round me;
    the horrors of the grave closed in on me;
I was filled with fear and anxiety.
    Then I called to the Lord,
'I beg you, Lord, save me!'

The Lord is merciful and good;
    our God is compassionate.
The Lord protects the helpless;
    when I was in danger, he saved me.
Be confident, my heart,
    because the Lord has been good to me.

The Lord saved me from death;
    he stopped my tears

and kept me from defeat.
    And so I walk in the presence of the Lord
in the world of the living.
    I kept on believing, even when I said,
'I am completely crushed,'
    even when I was afraid and said,
'No one can be trusted.'

What can I offer the Lord
    for all his goodness to me?
I will bring a wine offering to the Lord,
    to thank him for saving me.
In the assembly of all his people
    I will give him what I have promised.

How painful it is to the Lord
    when one of his people dies!
I am your servant, Lord;
    I serve you, just as my mother did.
You have saved me from death.
    I will give you a sacrifice of thanksgiving
and offer my prayer to you.
    In the assembly of all your people,
in the sanctuary of your Temple in Jerusalem,
    I will give you what I have promised.

Praise the Lord!

A widow at 23

ALBERT PENN

London Regiment (Post Office Rifles)

IT SHOULD HAVE BEEN THE HAPPIEST TIME OF THEIR LIVES. ALBERT AND
FLORENCE PENN, FROM THE VILLAGE OF HASLAND, NEAR CHESTERFIELD,
HAD NOT LONG BEEN MARRIED AND WERE EXPECTING THEIR FIRST
CHILD.

They had met at the Wesleyan Methodist Chapel in the village,
where he ran the boys' Bible class and she ran the equivalent for
girls. Devout and sincere Christians, their lives were focussed
around the little chapel and, now, their home.

But the war changed all that. Albert volunteered in 1916 and at
first he was refused because Florence was pregnant. 'Come back
when the baby is three months old,' he was told – so he did. Eight
months later, when baby Mary Estelle was just 11 months old, he
was dead.

Albert died at Passchendaele on 30 October 1917. He was 28
years old. His body was never found and his name is listed on teh
Tynecot Memorial to the missing, near Ypres.

Albert's granddaughter, Cynthia Hardiman, explains how a last
story about Albert brought solace to his bereaved wife Florence.
Just a few days before Albert and his regiment went over the top,
a member of his Bible class from home was being stretchered
away from the front and saw Albert.

'My grandfather was standing outside in the open field
with Bible in hand finishing a talk to the young soldiers,' says
Cynthia. 'He then led them in singing the hymn Rejoice the
Lord is King, your Lord and King adore.

'That was something really good for my grandmother to hang on to,' she says. 'She knew that he was still at heart the leader of the young men's Bible class – to the very end. Florence channelled her activities into the church. She always said that he was a better Christian than she was. His faith was very important to him. But they were both concerned about young people and getting them to know God.'

Nearly a century later, the preaching gene is still evident in Albert's family. Cynthia was a Methodist minister until retirement and married a Baptist minister.

'In a war, he was still preaching,' she says. 'He was still encouraging young fellas and trying to keep up morale. I like to think that, in that terrible time, he didn't keep the faith, the faith kept him.'

RUPERT BROOKE
Peace

Now, God be thanked Who has matched us with His hour,
And caught our youth, and wakened us from sleeping,
With hand made sure, clear eye, and sharpened power,
To turn, as swimmers into cleanness leaping,
Glad from a world grown old and cold and weary,
Leave the sick hearts that honour could not move,
And half-men, and their dirty songs and dreary,
And all the little emptiness of love!

Oh! we, who have known shame, we have found release there,
Where there's no ill, no grief, but sleep has mending,
Naught broken save this body, lost but breath;
Nothing to shake the laughing heart's long peace there
But only agony, and that has ending;
And the worst friend and enemy is but Death.

Prayer

Lord, make me an instrument of your peace.
Where there is hatred, let me sow love;
where there is injury, pardon;
where there is doubt, faith;
where there is despair, hope;
where there is darkness, light;
where there is sadness, joy.

O, divine master, grant that I may not so much seek
to be consoled as to console;
to be understood as to understand;
to be loved as to love;
for it is in giving that we receive;
it is in pardoning that we are pardoned;
and it is in dying that we are born to eternal life.
Amen.

Psalm 117

PRAISE THE LORD, ALL NATIONS!
   Praise him, all peoples!
His love for us is strong
   and his faithfulness is eternal.

Praise the Lord!

Prayer

Let us pray for all who suffer as a result of war:
for the injured and the disabled,
for the mentally distressed,
and for those whose faith in God and in man has been
weakened or destroyed …
for the homeless and refugees,
for those who are hungry,
and for all who have lost their livelihood and security …
for those who mourn their dead,
those who have lost husband or wife, children or parents,
and especially for those who have no hope in Christ to sustain
them in their grief …

Almighty God, our heavenly Father, infinite in wisdom, love and power:
have compassion on those for whom we pray; and help us to use all
suffering in the cause of your kingdom, through him who gave himself
for us on the cross, Jesus Christ your Son our Lord.
Amen.

Psalm 119

HOW CAN YOUNG PEOPLE KEEP THEIR LIVES PURE?
    By obeying your commands.
With all my heart I try to serve you;
    keep me from disobeying your commandments.
I keep your law in my heart,
    so that I will not sin against you.
I praise you, O Lord;
    teach me your ways.
I will repeat aloud
    all the laws you have given.
I delight in following your commands
    more than in having great wealth.
I study your instructions;
    I examine your teachings.
I take pleasure in your laws;
    your commands I will not forget. [...]

Show me how much you love me, Lord,
    and save me according to your promise.
Then I can answer those who insult me
    because I trust in your word.
Enable me to speak the truth at all times,
    because my hope is in your judgements.
I will always obey your law,
    for ever and ever.
I will live in perfect freedom,
    because I try to obey your teachings.
I will announce your commands to kings
    and I will not be ashamed.
I find pleasure in obeying your commands,
    because I love them.

I respect and love your commandments;
    I will meditate on your instructions. [...]

Your word is a lamp to guide me
    and a light for my path.
I will keep my solemn promise
    to obey your just instructions.
My sufferings, Lord, are terrible indeed;
    keep me alive, as you have promised.
Accept my prayer of thanks, O Lord,
    and teach me your commands.
I am always ready to risk my life;
    I have not forgotten your law.
The wicked lay a trap for me,
    but I have not disobeyed your commands.
Your commandments are my eternal possession;
    they are the joy of my heart.
I have decided to obey your laws
    until the day I die. [...]

WILFRED OWEN

The parable of the old man and the young

So Abram rose, and clave the wood, and went,
And took the fire with him, and a knife.
And as they sojourned both of them together,
Isaac the first-born spake and said, My Father,
Behold the preparations, fire and iron,
But where the lamb for this burnt-offering?
Then Abram bound the youth with belts and straps,
and builded parapets and trenches there,
And stretched forth the knife to slay his son.
When lo! an angel called him out of heaven,
Saying, Lay not thy hand upon the lad,
Neither do anything to him. Behold,
A ram, caught in a thicket by its horns;
Offer the Ram of Pride instead of him.

But the old man would not so, but slew his son,
And half the seed of Europe, one by one.

SIEGFRIED SASSOON
Attack

At dawn the ridge emerges massed and dun
In the wild purple of the glow'ring sun,
Smouldering through spouts of drifting smoke that shroud
The menacing scarred slope; and, one by one,
Tanks creep and topple forward to the wire.
The barrage roars and lifts. Then, clumsily bowed
With bombs and guns and shovels and battle-gear,
Men jostle and climb to meet the bristling fire.
Lines of grey, muttering faces, masked with fear,
They leave their trenches, going over the top,
While time ticks blank and busy on their wrists,
And hope, with furtive eyes and grappling fists,
Flounders in mud. O Jesus, make it stop!

Psalm 121

I LOOK TO THE MOUNTAINS;
where will my help come from?
     My help will come from the Lord,
who made heaven and earth.

He will not let you fall;
     your protector is always awake.
The protector of Israel
     never dozes or sleeps.
The Lord will guard you;
     he is by your side to protect you.
The sun will not hurt you during the day,
     nor the moon during the night.

The Lord will protect you from all danger;
     he will keep you safe.
He will protect you as you come and go
     now and for ever.

Psalm 124

WHAT IF THE LORD HAD NOT BEEN ON OUR SIDE?
    Answer, O Israel!

'If the Lord had not been on our side
    when our enemies attacked us,
then they would have swallowed us alive
    in their furious anger against us;
then the flood would have carried us away,
    the water would have covered us,
the raging torrent would have drowned us.'

Let us thank the Lord,
    who has not let our enemies destroy us.
We have escaped like a bird from a hunter's trap;
    the trap is broken, and we are free!
Our help comes from the Lord,
    who made heaven and earth.

Prayer

We believe in God,
God the Holy One,
God the Maker,
God who woke the clays of a cold earth to life,
God who glories in men and women,
children of his love.

We debased his holy will
and sowed the seeds of pain and death.

Yet in his steadfast love God pitied us;
he came to us in Jesus Christ,
his own dear Son,
our joy and gladness.

Seed, though dead and fallen,
burst to life and rose again,
our resurrection.

God breathes eternity into our souls,
and makes us flames of heaven's fire,
for the healing of the nations.

And so we bless and glorify his holy name.
In life, in death,
beyond life, beyond death,
God is with us.

Thanks be to God.
Amen.

Psalm 127

IF THE LORD DOES NOT BUILD THE HOUSE,
    the work of the builders is useless;
if the Lord does not protect the city,
    it is useless for the sentries to stand guard.
It is useless to work so hard for a living,
    getting up early and going to bed late.
For the Lord provides for those he loves,
    while they are asleep.

Children are a gift from the Lord;
    they are a real blessing.
The sons a man has when he is young
    are like arrows in a soldier's hand.
Happy is the man who has many such arrows.
    He will never be defeated
when he meets his enemies in the place of judgement.

Box Brownie war record

SHELTON FROST

Army Service Corps

SHELTON FROST, A FARM LABOURER FROM LINCOLNSHIRE, WAS 'A VISIONARY' ACCORDING TO HIS GRANDDAUGHTERS SHEILA RICHARDSON AND JOY ROBINSON.

PHOTOS: BIBLE SOCIETY/CLARE KENDALL

'When he was a young man, he decided that the motor car was the future,' says Sheila. 'So he took himself off to Manchester to take a driving course.'

The result was that, when World War One broke out, 25-year-old Shelton enlisted in the Army Service Corps and found himself first in Egypt and then Palestine.

A committed Christian and regular churchgoer, he took with him a small black New Testament, one of millions printed by the Bible Society. Inside the front cover is his name with the legend 'Alexandria October 28 1916'.

Shelton had 'a quiet faith' that 'never wavered' despite his war experiences, Sheila says.

'To have been thrown into a country on the other side of the world, with different terrain, where it's dry and dusty and with temperatures that he'd never experienced, separated

from his family, I would imagine it would have been very important to him to be reading his Bible.'

Because of Shelton's love of photography, it's possible to look back 100 years and see snapshots of his war experience. He took with him a Box Brownie, which still works today, and took hundreds of photographs, now stored in shoeboxes. There are shots of Shelton at sites that he'd have read about in the Bible, including Jacob's Well, and packs of photographs bought in the early tourist trade, showing biblical sites in Jerusalem.

Pictures of lorries that have come off what passed for roads across the desert (shown above) hint at the difficulties of the work that Shelton faced.

But there is also a lighter side, the camaraderie, with a picture of his colleagues ranged in a tall row looking out of a tent (see page 30), and a splendid shot of Shelton in uniform and pith helmet on a camel in front of the pyramids.

'Everybody says that being in the Holy Land really speaks to you,' says Sheila. 'So for him to be in the places that he was reading about in the Bible, it must have spoken to him a great deal.'

Psalm 128

HAPPY ARE THOSE WHO OBEY THE LORD,
    who live by his commands.

Your work will provide for your needs;
    you will be happy and prosperous.
Your wife will be like a fruitful vine in your home,
    and your children will be like young olive trees round your
        table.
A man who obeys the Lord
    will surely be blessed like this.

May the Lord bless you from Zion!
    May you see Jerusalem prosper
all the days of your life!
    May you live to see your grandchildren!

Peace be with Israel!

Psalm 130

FROM THE DEPTHS OF MY DESPAIR I CALL TO YOU,
    LORD.
    Hear my cry, O Lord;
listen to my call for help!
    If you kept a record of our sins,
who could escape being condemned?
    But you forgive us,
so that we should stand in awe of you.

I wait eagerly for the Lord's help,
    and in his word I trust.
I wait for the Lord
    more eagerly than watchmen wait for the dawn —
than watchmen wait for the dawn.

Israel, trust in the Lord,
    because his love is constant
and he is always willing to save.
    He will save his people Israel
from all their sins.

ISAAC ROSENBERG

Returning we hear the larks

Sombre the night is.
And though we have our lives, we know
What sinister threat lies there.

Dragging these anguished limbs, we only know
This poison-blasted track opens on our camp –
On a little safe sleep.

But hark! joy – joy – strange joy.
Lo! heights of night ringing with unseen larks.
Music showering our upturned list'ning faces.

Death could drop from the dark
As easily as song –
But song only dropped,
Like a blind man's dreams on the sand
By dangerous tides,
Like a girl's dark hair for she dreams no ruin lies there,
Or her kisses where a serpent hides.

R E VERNÈDE

A listening post

The sun's a red ball in the oak
And all the grass is grey with dew,
A while ago a blackbird spoke –
He didn't know the world's askew

And yonder rifleman and I
Wait here behind the misty trees
To shoot the first man that goes by,
Our rifles ready on our knees.

How could he know that if we fail
The world may lie in chains for years
And England be a bygone tale
And right be wrong, and laughter tears?

Strange that this bird sits there and sings
While we must only sit and plan –
Who are so much the higher things –
The murder of our fellow man.

But maybe God will cause to be –
Who brought forth sweetness from the strong –
Out of our discords harmony
Sweeter than that bird's song.

Psalm 131

LORD, I HAVE GIVEN UP MY PRIDE
  and turned away from my arrogance.
I am not concerned with great matters
  or with subjects too difficult for me.
Instead, I am content and at peace.
  As a child lies quietly in its mother's arms,
so my heart is quiet within me.
  Israel, trust in the Lord
now and for ever!

Psalm 133

HOW WONDERFUL IT IS, HOW PLEASANT,
   for God's people to live together in harmony!
It is like the precious anointing oil
   running down from Aaron's head and beard,
down to the collar of his robes.
   It is like the dew on Mount Hermon,
falling on the hills of Zion.
   That is where the Lord has promised his blessing —
life that never ends.

Psalm 137

BY THE RIVERS OF BABYLON WE SAT DOWN;
    there we wept when we remembered Zion.
On the willows near by
    we hung up our harps.
Those who captured us told us to sing;
    they told us to entertain them:
'Sing us a song about Zion.'

How can we sing a song to the Lord
    in a foreign land?
May I never be able to play the harp again
    if I forget you, Jerusalem!
May I never be able to sing again
    if I do not remember you,
if I do not think of you as my greatest joy!

Remember, Lord, what the Edomites did
    the day Jerusalem was captured.
Remember how they kept saying,
    'Tear it down to the ground!'

Babylon, you will be destroyed.
    Happy are those who pay you back
for what you have done to us —
    who take your babies
and smash them against a rock.

Psalm 138

I THANK YOU, LORD, WITH ALL MY HEART;
   I sing praise to you before the gods.
I face your holy Temple,
   bow down, and praise your name
because of your constant love and faithfulness,
   because you have shown that your name and your commands
      are supreme.
You answered me when I called to you;
   with your strength you strengthened me.

All the kings in the world will praise you, Lord,
   because they have heard your promises.
They will sing about what you have done
   and about your great glory.
Even though you are so high above,
   you care for the lowly,
and the proud cannot hide from you.

When I am surrounded by troubles,
   you keep me safe.
You oppose my angry enemies
   and save me by your power.
You will do everything you have promised;
   Lord, your love is eternal.
Complete the work that you have begun.

Too old for active service?

THOMAS WINTER

YMCA

'WHEN WAR BROKE OUT, MY OWN GREAT-GRANDFATHER THOMAS WINTER KNEW HE HAD TO BE THERE,' WRITES HAZEL SOUTHAM OF BIBLE SOCIETY, WHO HAS RESEARCHED ALL THE ORIGINAL STORIES IN THIS BOOK.

She goes on to tell the story of how, at 59, her great-grandfather was too old for active service. Instead he joined the YMCA to set up and run their social centres for soldiers away from the front line. Perhaps not surprisingly, all the soldiers called him 'Daddy'.

It was a remarkable action for a teacher-cum-farmer from a quiet village in the depths of Buckinghamshire's countryside – but it was in character, according to Hazel's mother, Mary Southam, who remembers Thomas Winter well.

'I was always brought up to think of him as a very fine old Christian man because he had spent his life doing what he thought he should for the kingdom of God,' she says. 'He was a man of the Baptist chapel in the village, leading the Sunday

PHOTOGRAPH OF BEARER

SIGNATURE OF BEARER.

Thomas Winter

School and helping to raise funds to expand the church. He was a very sociable and likeable person and wanted to do his bit in whatever way he could.'

In 1914, that meant leaving the farm that he ran on the outskirts of the village of Holmer Green and heading for France and then Italy.

His diaries provide an insight into his training for the YMCA, when he chose the same hymns that were being sung at his home church in Buckinghamshire. He was told that 'there is a chariot of fire about us' and that he was to 'be a witness for the truth'. As well as knowing that a 1lb jar of Bovril made 48 cups of drink, he was to 'help someone know they are saved'.

At first he found his work rather dull, until 7,000 men and 2,000 horses turned up and he was run off his feet. He built huts from scratch, and in Marseilles was asked by the officers to provide courts for tennis, baseball and badminton as well as a cricket pitch with netting. In Italy, he formed a choir of 40 men and led Sunday evening services and concerts on Friday nights.

'He was mature enough to be able to be a good friend and counsel to soldiers whom he met who were perhaps having a really rough time,' says my mother. I should think he was in a good place to use his Christian faith to comfort and strengthen those soldiers.'

Words for when there are no words 107

Psalm 139

**LORD, YOU HAVE EXAMINED ME AND YOU KNOW
ME.**

You know everything I do;
from far away you understand all my thoughts.
You see me, whether I am working or resting;
you know all my actions.
Even before I speak,
you already know what I will say.
You are all round me on every side;
you protect me with your power.
Your knowledge of me is too deep;
it is beyond my understanding.

Where could I go to escape from you?
Where could I get away from your presence?
If I went up to heaven, you would be there;
if I lay down in the world of the dead, you would be there.
If I flew away beyond the east
or lived in the farthest place in the west,
you would be there to lead me,
you would be there to help me.
I could ask the darkness to hide me
or the light round me to turn into night,
but even darkness is not dark for you,
and the night is as bright as the day.
Darkness and light are the same to you.

You created every part of me;
you put me together in my mother's womb.
I praise you because you are to be feared;
all you do is strange and wonderful.
I know it with all my heart.

When my bones were being formed,
    carefully put together in my mother's womb,
when I was growing there in secret,
    you knew that I was there —
you saw me before I was born.
    The days allotted to me
had all been recorded in your book,
    before any of them ever began.
O God, how difficult I find your thoughts;
    how many of them there are!
If I counted them, they would be more than the grains of sand.
    When I awake, I am still with you.

O God, how I wish you would kill the wicked!
    How I wish violent people would leave me alone!
They say wicked things about you;
    they speak evil things against your name.
O Lord, how I hate those who hate you!
    How I despise those who rebel against you!
I hate them with a total hatred;
    I regard them as my enemies.

Examine me, O God, and know my mind;
    test me, and discover my thoughts.
Find out if there is any evil in me
    and guide me in the everlasting way.

From WWI to Afghanistan

PRIVATE CURTIS WELSBY

The 1st Mercian Regiment

PHOTO: BIBLE SOCIETY/CLARE KENDALL

WHEN PTE CURTIS WELSBY'S FRIEND, JAMIE, DIED IN AFGHANISTAN JUST WEEKS BEFORE THEIR BATTALION WAS TO RETURN TO THE UK, THE 20-YEAR-OLD FROM MANCHESTER TURNED TO THE BIBLE. PTE WELSBY, FROM THE 1ST BATTALION THE MERCIAN REGIMENT, CARRIED AN ACTIVE SERVICE TESTAMENT FROM 1916 IN HIS BODY ARMOUR.

'I was upset, I was angry,' Pte Welsby recalls that time in March 2013. 'We all had our body armour on. I noticed the Bible popping out a little bit from my pocket. I went to put it back and then I thought, "No, I'm going to read it. I need something to make me feel good right now".'

Randomly, he found himself at Revelation and read in chapter 21 verse 4: 'And God shall wipe away all tears from their eyes; and there shall be no more death, neither sorrow, nor crying, neither shall there be any more pain: for the former things are passed away.'

'I read it over and over again,' he says. 'And I thought, there's nothing for Jamie to worry about now. It was exactly what I needed to read, because what happened was so totally devastating and unexpected.'

Pte Welsby's little New Testament has seen five conflicts.

It first belonged to his great-great grandfather, Jay Greenwood, a teenager who fought in the First World War having lied about his age. It was passed on to his great grandfather who took it with him to the battlefields of the Second World War. It then travelled to Korea with Pte Welsby's grandfather and to Northern Ireland with his Uncle.

Its thin pages are worn with use and it readily falls open both at Acts and John. But it was Revelation that spoke to Pte Welsby on his tour of Afghanistan. 'Arriving in Afghanistan was scary,' he recalls. 'When you leave Camp Bastion you realise that it's real. It's you and your friends now. I kept my Bible with me in my pocket all the time and it calmed me down. I thought that God would be looking down over me. I had a sense of Him being with me.

'I would pull it out and read it when we went on patrol and I had a tingling feeling go through my body every time. Anything could happen. Nobody had a clue what would happen. But, when I picked up my Bible, I felt that nothing would happen to us. We got into firefights, but we always got out of them.

'When we were out on patrols and we would stop, I would pull it out and the stories in there make you feel happy. I could read it all day. The local kids used to ask me for it but I always said "no". It's been in my family for so long. It'll be passed on to my nephew. He's only seven, but he already wants to be in the Army.'

All five generations of Pte Welsby's family have served in the Infantry, so it is perhaps surprising that both the Bible and men survived.

'It means a lot to me,' he says. 'All of my family has read it. I wish I could know what they read. But me and my granddad were very close and we both liked exactly the same things. I reckon he had a hand in saying, "Stop at that page". I reckon somehow he guided me to reading Revelation.'

WILFRED OWEN
Futility

Move him into the sun —
Gently its touch awoke him once,
At home, whispering of fields unsown.
Always it woke him, even in France,
Until this morning and this snow.
If anything might rouse him now
The kind old sun will know.

Think how it wakes the seeds, —
Woke, once, the clays of a cold star.
Are limbs, so dear-achieved, are sides,
Full-nerved — still warm — too hard to stir?
Was it for this the clay grew tall?
— O what made fatuous sunbeams toil
To break earth's sleep at all?

ELEANOR FARJEON
Easter Monday

In the last letter that I had from France
You thanked me for the silver Easter egg
Which I had hidden in the box of apples
You like to munch beyond all other fruit.
You found the egg the Monday before Easter,
And said. 'I will praise Easter Monday now –
It was such a lovely morning'. Then you spoke
Of the coming battle and said, 'This is the eve.
'Good-bye. And may I have a letter soon'.

That Easter Monday was a day for praise,
It was such a lovely morning. In our garden
We sowed our earliest seeds, and in the orchard
The apple-bud was ripe. It was the eve,
There are three letters that you will not get.

HYMN

Guide Me O Thou Great Redeemer

Guide me, O thou great redeemer,
Pilgrim through this barren land;
  I am weak, but thou art mighty,
    Hold me with thy powerful hand;
      Bread of heaven, bread of heaven
  Feed me till I want no more;
  Feed me till I want no more.

Open now the crystal fountain
Whence the healing stream doth flow;
  Let the fiery cloudy pillar
    Lead me all my journey through:
      Strong deliverer, strong deliverer;
Be thou still my strength and shield;
Be thou still my strength and shield.

When I tread the verge of Jordan,
Bid my anxious fears subside;
  Death of death, and hell's destruction
    Land me safe on Canaan's side:
      Songs of praises, songs of praises,
I will ever give to thee;
I will ever give to thee.

BRITISH SOLDIERS WOUNDED BY GAS
(SEE ALSO PAGE 64) PHOTO: AKG-IMAGES

Psalm 143

LORD, HEAR MY PRAYER!
   In your righteousness listen to my plea;
answer me in your faithfulness!
   Don't put me, your servant, on trial;
no one is innocent in your sight.

My enemies have hunted me down
   and completely defeated me.
They have put me in a dark prison,
   and I am like those who died long ago.
So I am ready to give up;
   I am in deep despair.

I remember the days gone by;
   I think about all that you have done,
I bring to mind all your deeds.
   I lift up my hands to you in prayer;
like dry ground my soul is thirsty for you.

Answer me now, Lord!
   I have lost all hope.
Don't hide yourself from me,

or I will be among those who go down to the world
        of the dead.
Remind me each morning of your constant love,
    for I put my trust in you.
My prayers go up to you;
    show me the way I should go.

I go to you for protection, Lord;
    rescue me from my enemies.
You are my God;
    teach me to do your will.
Be good to me, and guide me on a safe path.

Rescue me, Lord, as you have promised;
    in your goodness save me from my troubles!
Because of your love for me, kill my enemies
    and destroy all my oppressors,
for I am your servant.

Psalm 145

**I WILL PROCLAIM YOUR GREATNESS, MY GOD AND
    KING;**
    I will thank you for ever and ever.
Every day I will thank you;
    I will praise you for ever and ever.
The Lord is great and is to be highly praised;
    his greatness is beyond understanding.

What you have done will be praised from one generation to the
    next;
    they will proclaim your mighty acts.
They will speak of your glory and majesty,
    and I will meditate on your wonderful deeds.
People will speak of your mighty deeds,
    and I will proclaim your greatness.
They will tell about all your goodness
    and sing about your kindness.
The Lord is loving and merciful,
    slow to become angry and full of constant love.
He is good to everyone
    and has compassion on all he made.

All your creatures, Lord, will praise you,
    and all your people will give you thanks.
They will speak of the glory of your royal power
    and tell of your might,
so that everyone will know your mighty deeds
    and the glorious majesty of your kingdom.
Your rule is eternal,
    and you are king for ever.

The Lord is faithful to his promises,
and he is merciful in all his acts.
He helps those who are in trouble;
he lifts those who have fallen.

All living things look hopefully to you,
and you give them food when they need it.
You give them enough
and satisfy the needs of all.

The Lord is righteous in all he does,
merciful in all his acts.
He is near to those who call to him,
who call to him with sincerity.
He supplies the needs of those who honour him;
he hears their cries and saves them.
He protects everyone who loves him,
but he will destroy the wicked.

I will always praise the Lord;
let all his creatures praise his holy name for ever.

The Bible saved his life

ARTHUR INGHAM

Manchester Regiment

ARTHUR INGHAM AND JOHN MOODY WERE 18-YEAR-OLD SCHOOL FRIENDS WHO'D GROWN UP IN MANCHESTER TOGETHER. WHEN WAR BROKE OUT, THE TWO LADS JOINED UP AT MANCHESTER TOWN HALL.

Like many young men they joined local regiments that drew in people who all lived in one area or came from one workplace.

Sent to the front in France, they were both involved in the Battle of the Somme. And it was here that the little Bible that Arthur kept in his top pocket saved his life.

He was in the 1st Manchester Regiment at the Somme, when an exploding German shell sent a piece of shrapnel flying towards him. It hit his chest and would have meant certain death had he not had his Bible in the breast pocket of his uniform.

It took the full force of the shrapnel, which left an inch-wide hole.

John's son Philip Douetil remembers Arthur well. 'He was such a fantastic bloke,' he says. 'And he was really proud of this Bible. He used to say to me, "This saved my life. If it hadn't been in my pocket, I would have died." ' The shrapnel also made a mess of

Arthur's uniform, resulting in a 'telling off' from an officer for 'not looking after his uniform properly,' says Philip.

The incident changed Arthur's life. 'He was a religious man after that,' Philip recalls. 'He wasn't beforehand, but after that he became a regular churchgoer, and who can blame him? He knew the Bible had saved his life. The shrapnel had hit but there wasn't a scratch on him.'

Psalm 146

PRAISE THE LORD!
　Praise the Lord, my soul!
I will praise him as long as I live;
　I will sing to my God all my life.

Don't put your trust in human leaders;
　no human being can save you.
When they die, they return to the dust;
　on that day all their plans come to an end.

Happy are those who have the God of Jacob to help them
　and who depend on the Lord their God,
the Creator of heaven, earth, and sea,
　and all that is in them.
He always keeps his promises;
　he judges in favour of the oppressed
and gives food to the hungry.

The Lord sets prisoners free
　and gives sight to the blind.
He lifts those who have fallen;
　he loves his righteous people.
He protects the strangers who live in our land;
　he helps widows and orphans,
but takes the wicked to their ruin.

The Lord is king for ever.
　Your God, O Zion, will reign for all time.

Praise the Lord!

Psalm 150

Praise God in his Temple!
    Praise his strength in heaven!
Praise him for the mighty things he has done.
    Praise his supreme greatness.

Praise him with trumpets.
    Praise him with harps and lyres.
Praise him with drums and dancing.
    Praise him with harps and flutes.
Praise him with cymbals.
    Praise him with loud cymbals.
Praise the Lord, all living creatures!

Praise the Lord!

A matter of seconds

GEORGE HEVER VINALL

Royal Artillery

17 JULY 1915

DEAR MOTHER AND FATHER

I AM SENDING IN A PARCEL, MY POCKET BIBLE AND THREE SHRAPNEL
BULLETS, OF WHICH THE FOLLOWING IS THE STORY.

Last Thursday, just before midday, I returned to my sleeping
apartment and threw off my tunic and respirator, laid my bundle of
kit down for a pillow and intended having a little rest.

I was looking round for something to read when I saw a friend
coming along so I went round to the door to speak to him. Just as
I went to the door a shell exploded somewhere in the grounds
and Gibson (who sleeps next to me) started off to the horse lines
thinking there might be trouble there.

A BOMBARDIER'S MIRACULOUS
ESCAPE.

AN AVIARY AS SLEEPING PLACE.

AMONGST THE GAS SHELLS.

Below are extracts from two letters received from
Bombardier G. H. Vinall by his parents, Mr. and Mrs.
Clement J. Vinall, Erlesdene, Upper-avenue, East-
bourne. Bombardier Vinall, who was for some years a
member of the 4th Sussex Battery (Eastbourne),
R.F.A., is now connected with the West Riding
Division, R.A., and is serving with the Expeditionary
Force in France.

Writing on July 15th, he says:—

Very many thanks for the parcel of chocolate which
arrived safely a day or two ago. They were very
which arrived safely a day or two ago. They were very
nice and we have enjoyed them very much with

He had hardly gone when we heard another coming and immediately got down flat on the floor behind the brick pillar, a sprinkling of dust and wood splinters fell round us as the shell burst outside. That was enough for us. We got up and ran for a trench nearby and as soon as we heard the next coming we flattened ourselves at the bottom, not troubling about the dirt so long as we could get under cover and so we remained until it was over.

When I returned for my tunic and respirator, we discovered that about a dozen men had been wounded, two of whom subsequently died. As far as we could trace, four bullets came in, one being embedded in my kit where my head would have been but for the arrival of my friend. Another was on the floor where I would have been lying. The third was in the pocket of my tunic having been stopped by my Bible, as you can see, and the fourth went through Gibson's mackintosh which was hung up in the compartment next to mine, where he would have been had he not started off a few seconds before for the horse lines.

So you see our escape was only a matter of seconds. How quickly I have had to prove the truth of what I said in my last letter, 'safe in the hands' and yet such is the case that I am here without a scratch, safe and well. The eighth verse of Isaiah 49, where the bullet stopped, contains these words which caught my eye directly I saw it, 'I will preserve thee'. May this be true of future days until I see you all again is my heartfelt prayer.

Your loving son
George

LUCY WHITMELL

Christ in Flanders

We had forgotten You, or very nearly —
You did not seem to touch us very nearly —
Of course we thought about You now and then;
Especially in any time of trouble —
We knew that You were good in time of trouble —
But we are very ordinary men.

And there were always other things to think of —
There's lots of things a man has got to think of —
His work, his home, his pleasure, and his wife;
And so we only thought of You on Sunday —
Sometimes, perhaps, not even on a Sunday —
Because there's always lots to fill one's life.

And, all the while, in street or lane or byway —
In country lane, in city street, or byway —
You walked among us, and we did not see.
Your feet were bleeding as You walked our pavements —
How did we miss Your footprints on our pavements? —
Can there be other folk as blind as we?

Now we remember; over here in Flanders —
(It isn't strange to think of You in Flanders) —
This hideous warfare seems to make things clear.
We never thought about You much in England —
But now that we are far away from England,
We have no doubts, we know that You are here.

You helped us pass the jest along the trenches —
Where, in cold blood, we waited in the trenches —

You touched its ribaldry and made it fine.
You stood beside us in our pain and weakness —
We're glad to think You understand our weakness —
Somehow it seems to help us not to whine.

We think about You kneeling in the Garden —
Ah! God! the agony of that dread Garden —
We know You prayed for us upon the cross.
If anything could make us glad to bear it —
'Twould be the knowledge that You willed to bear it —
Pain — death — the uttermost of human loss.

Though we forgot You — You will not forget us —
We feel so sure that You will not forget us —
But stay with us until this dream is past.
And so we ask for courage, strength, and pardon —
Especially, I think, we ask for pardon —
And that You'll stand beside us to the last.

ROBERT GRAVES

The last post

The bugler sent a call of high romance —
'Lights out! Lights out!' to the deserted square.
On the thin brazen notes he threw a prayer,
'God, if it's this for me next time in France …
O spare the phantom bugle as I lie
Dead in the gas and smoke and roar of guns,
Dead in a row with the other broken ones
Lying so stiff and still under the sky,
Jolly young Fusiliers too good to die.'

Prayer

Our Father in heaven,
hallowed be your name.
Your kingdom come,
your will be done,
on earth as in heaven
Give us today our daily bread.
Forgive us our sins,
as we forgive those who sin against us.
Lead us not into temptation,
but deliver us from evil.
For the kingdom,
the power and the glory are yours.
Now and for ever.
Amen.

References

Beyond Our Tears: resources for times of remembrance, edited by Jean
M Mayland, published by Churches Together in Britain and Ireland,
2004.

Contemporary Parish Prayers by Frank Colquhoun, published by Hodder &
Stoughton, 1975.

Forgotten Voices of the Great War, by Max Arthur in association with the
Imperial War Museum, published by Ebury Press, 2003.

The Lion Prayer Collection selected and arranged by Mary Batchelor,
published by Lion Publishing plc, 1992.

Parish Prayers, edited by Frank Colquhoun, published by Hodder &
Stoughton, 1967.

Up the Line to Death, The War Poets 1914–18, an anthology by Brian Gardner,
published by Methuen & Co Ltd, 1964.

Acknowledgements

Grateful thanks go to Sister Wendy Beckett for generously writing the
commentaries on pages 64 and 69 specially for this volume.

Stories researched and written by Hazel Southam © 2014 The British and
Foreign Bible Society.

Stories and original images used with kind permission of: Dr Foster
(Harry Foster), Mr John Young (Walter Young), Mr Anthony Hasler
(Cyril Mead), Miss Violet Culliford (Walter Culliford), Mrs Sheila
Richardson (Shelton Frost), Mrs Wendy Kellaway (Theo Chadburn),
Mr David Winter (Thomas Winter), Pte Curtis Welsby, Mrs Cynthia
Hardiman (Albert Penn), Mr Philip Douetil (Arthur Ingham); John Harris,
Bible Society of Australia (Elvas Jenkins).

Extracts by Private Godfrey Buxton and Trooper George Jameson
taken from *Forgotten Voices of the Great War* by Max Arthur, used with kind
permission of Imperial War Museum and Random House Publishers.

The Bibles pictured on pages 110 and 121 were originally published
during the First World War by the Naval, Military and Air Force Bible
Society.

Poems:

'A Dirge of Victory' by Lord Dunsany reproduced with permission of Curtis Brown Group Ltd, London, on behalf of The Estate of Lord Dunsany. Copyright © Lord Dunsany 1929.

'Perhaps' by Vera Brittain is included by permission of Mark Bostridge and T J Brittain-Catlin, Literary Executors for the Estate of Vera Brittain 1970.

'Attack' by Siegried Sassoon, copyright © Siegried Sassoon and reproduced by kind permission of the Estate of George Sassoon.

'The Last Post' by Robert Graves from *Complete Poems in One Volume* by Robert Graves, Carcanet Press Ltd 2001, with permission of Carcanet Press Ltd.

'Easter Monday' by Eleanor Farjeon from *The New Book of Days,* Oxford University Press 1941, with permission of David Higham Associates.

Hymns:

'O God our help in ages past', Isaac Watts, 1719; 'Lead us heavenly father, lead us', James Edmeston, 1821; 'Guide me O thou great redeemer', William Williams, translated from the Welsh by Peter Williams, 1771.

Prayers:

Page 7; page 87 from the Service of Remembrance; taken from *Contemporary Parish Prayers* by Frank Colquhoun, Hodder & Stoughton. used with kind permission of Hodder Publishing Ltd.

Page 33 copyright CTBI Group; page 94 copyright Fleur Houston; taken from *Beyond Our Tears*, edited by Jean M Mayland, Churches Together in Britain and Ireland, used with kind permission of the Joint Liturgical Group and Churches Together in Britain and Ireland and with kind permission of Fleur Houston.

Page 43 copyright Baptist Peace Fellowship, taken from *The Lion Prayer Collection*, Mary Batchelor, Lion Publishing, used with kind permission of Baptist Peace Fellowship

Page 79 copyright Alan Paton, taken from *Instrument of Thy Peace*, Seabury Press, used with kind permission of the Alan Paton Will Trust.

Page 85 by Anonymous 1915; page 129 the Lord's Prayer modern version.

Every effort has been made to trace copyright holders and to obtain permission for the use of copyright material. The publisher apologises for any errors or omissions and would be grateful if notified of any corrections to be incorporated in any future reprints or editions of this book.

With gratitude also to Sue Coyne and Dorothy Mountford at www.crossref-it.info and Dr Michael Snape, University of Birmingham.

1914
WWI CENTENARY
1918

The 4th of August 2014 marks the 100th anniversary of the day Britain entered one of the costliest conflicts in history – the First World War – which ended on the 11th of November 1918, Armistice Day.

Nearly everyone in the UK has an ancestor directly affected by the First World War and all of us live with its effects today. The losses were felt in nearly every UK town and village as more than 1.1 million lives were sacrificed by men and women in service of the British Empire.

The Royal British Legion was founded by British veterans in the aftermath of the First World War and will be at the forefront of Centenary commemorations. As we come together in Remembrance of events a century ago, we are reminded of the important welfare work the Legion continues to provide today and will need to provide in the future.

A century on from the First World War, those serving in the Armed Forces, veterans and their families still call on us for help with almost every aspect of daily life. The problems facing First World War veterans when they returned to the UK continue to affect serving personnel and veterans today: whether living with bereavement or disability, finding employment, or coping with financial stress.

As the UK's Custodian of Remembrance, the Legion will be leading the nation in respecting the sacrifices of the First World War. As the UK's largest Armed Forces charity, the Legion will be leading the nation in providing direct care and support to Armed Forces and veteran families in need.

Help us to catch the torch from the First World War fallen to hold it high today. Visit **britishlegion.org.uk**